TIME FOR KIDS READERS

AF571933

THE ELGIN MARBLES

by Anna Prokos

Orlando Austin Chicago New York Toronto London San Diego

Visit *The Learning Site!*
www.harcourtschool.com

More than 2,400 years ago—a sculptor named Phidias was the pride of ancient Greece. Along with the architects Ictinus and Callicrates, he designed the magnificent marble temple, the Parthenon. It still stands today on the Acropolis, a central hill in Athens. Never in his wildest dreams could he have imagined that, a thousand years later, parts of his building would end up more than 1,500 miles (2,400 km) away. But that's exactly what happened.

Now fast-forward to 1800. That was the year Thomas Bruce, the British Earl of Elgin, began his quest for Greek art. The result was that the Parthenon lost many of its marbles, or at least many of its marble statues.

The Acropolis still rises over Athens.

Lord Elgin

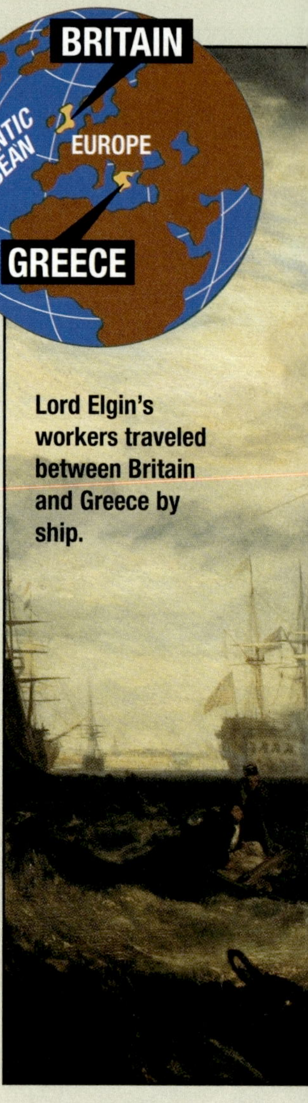

Lord Elgin's workers traveled between Britain and Greece by ship.

Lord Elgin's big idea came to him in 1796 while he was fixing up his house. The architect who was working on it mentioned that classical Greek art was becoming very popular. He told Elgin that all the "best" people in Britain were copying Greek buildings like the Parthenon for their own homes.

Elgin wanted a copy of the Parthenon that was as close to the real thing as possible, based on an exact cast of the temple. To get permission to make a cast, Elgin decided to use his political connections. It helped that Elgin was the British ambassador to the Ottoman Empire. It ruled Greece, among other countries. Surely the Ottoman Empire would allow him to make casts of the buildings on the Acropolis, Elgin thought. So he gathered a team of 300 workers and sent them to Athens. The workers were equipped with ropes, scaffolds, and plaster. But Elgin himself couldn't go with them. He couldn't leave his duties as ambassador. He sent his friend Philip Hunt to lead the team.

When Hunt and his team arrived in Athens, they marched right up to the Parthenon to start working. But they were turned away. Ottoman soldiers said the workers would need a special permit to make casts of the Parthenon. The permit, called a *firman*, had to come directly from Ottoman headquarters.

It took 10 months of letter-writing by Lord Elgin to receive the firman. He had asked only for permission to make casts. The firman gave him more. It said: "When they [the English] wish to take away any pieces of stone with inscriptions or figures, no hindrance or opposition be made thereto." Elgin was overjoyed! Who needed casts when he could get the real thing?

That's where the firman got tricky—and how the fight for the Elgin Marbles began. Lord Elgin never intended to break off pieces of the original monument.

He thought his team had permission to remove fallen pieces of the Parthenon and bring them back to England. But Hunt interpreted the firman differently. He convinced the Ottoman soldiers that the permit allowed him to take away sculptures that were still on the Parthenon. Because of this, the soldiers gave him permission to remove one of the Parthenon's metopes. The metopes (MEH•tuh•peez) were a series of marble sculptures that told mythological stories. The next day, Hunt sawed off another metope. Athenians and local authorities protested. Hunt pointed to the firman. Here, he said, was proof that he could take anything and everything he wanted.

This is part of the eastern frieze of the Parthenon.

Why did Hunt do this? He insisted he was saving the sculptures from total destruction. The Ottoman military was smashing up columns and sculptures on a daily basis. They were looking for lead pieces the ancient Greeks had put into the marble. The soldiers planned to use the lead to make ammunition. In addition, Hunt told Elgin, travelers who visited the Parthenon broke off pieces of the monument for souvenirs. Hunt convinced Elgin that if the destruction continued, little of the Parthenon would be left standing.

With that in mind, the team removed as much as possible from the Parthenon and other buildings on the Acropolis. Batches of artifacts were loaded onto British boats bound for England. But not every boat made it back to England. One was captured by the French navy. Another sank two days into its journey. Though all the marbles eventually reached England, the event was the beginning of trouble for Lord Elgin.

During the early 1800s Britain and France were at war. In 1803 while visiting France, Lord Elgin was arrested. Napoleon Bonaparte, the ruler of France, tried to bargain with Elgin. In exchange for the marbles, Elgin could have his freedom. Lord Elgin wouldn't budge.

France released Lord Elgin in 1806. On his return home, he found that several tons of his prized artwork had been sitting in a British port for more than two years. The shipment had 56 panels from the frieze, or decorated border, 15 metopes, 17 statues, and several other pieces of architecture.

Transporting the marbles to Britain had cost Lord Elgin a great deal of money. He soon decided to try to sell the marbles to the British government. But his price was too high. The government refused the offer. Elgin spent four years trying to find a buyer for the marbles. In 1816 Elgin finally settled for the British government's offer: less than half his original asking price. Since then, the Parthenon Marbles, also known as the Elgin Marbles, have been housed in the British Museum, and are at the center of a centuries-old fight.

A Greek politician once called these marbles "the essence of Greekness."

TFK
DID YOU KNOW

The Man Behind the Marbles

If he hadn't taken the Parthenon marbles, Lord Elgin probably wouldn't be famous. Born on July 20, 1766, Thomas Bruce was the son of Charles Bruce, the fifth Earl of Elgin. When Thomas was only five years old he gained the title of seventh Earl of Elgin from his brother, William Robert Bruce.

In 1785 Lord Elgin began a military career, rising to the rank of major general. It was at this time that he became interested in politics. As Lord Elgin, he was able to join the House of Lords. That's the part of the British Parliament with representatives who are born or named to their positions rather than elected. The House of Commons is made up of elected representatives.

In 1790 Lord Elgin became a diplomat for the British government. Diplomats represent their governments in other countries. He served in Belgium and Germany before being sent to Constantinople, in what is today Turkey. It was while Lord Elgin was working in Constantinople that he arranged to remove the marbles from the Parthenon.

When he finally collected the marbles in 1806, Lord Elgin was deeply in debt. In 1816 the British government agreed to buy the marbles for 35,000 pounds. Although this helped him pay his debts, it was much less than he wanted to accept. Lord Elgin died in Paris, France, in 1841.

The Elgin Marbles are housed in the British Museum.

The disagreement between Greece and Britain has lasted close to 200 years. Greece and other countries have been asking Britain to return the marbles to their original home at the Acropolis. But Britain says it purchased the marbles from Lord Elgin, who was given permission to take them. In the past 20 years, Greece has stepped up its effort to get back the marbles.

During planning for the 2004 Olympic Games in Athens, the Greek government asked to borrow the marbles. That would allow visitors to see the pieces of the Parthenon together in one place. Though Britain has refused in the past, it has not yet given a decision. Greece remains hopeful. The Greeks are planning to build the New Acropolis Museum, a state-of-the-art facility built just for the marbles' return.

TFK

DID YOU KNOW

"WE WANT OUR MARBLES BACK!"

Since 1817 Greece has been asking Britain to return the marbles to the Parthenon. The Greeks say Lord Elgin and his team stole the marbles. They believe that Hunt bribed Ottoman authorities and that the Ottomans did not have the right to give up pieces of Greek monuments. They also argue that the sculptures were meant to be viewed as part of a building—not in a museum. People who support the return of the marbles believe Britain has a moral obligation to give back the marbles to the people of Greece, whose cultural past is chiseled into the rock.

"THE MARBLES ARE STAYING PUT!"

More than 6 million people have seen the Elgin Marbles in the British Museum—and that's where the marbles are going to stay, say British authorities. They point to historic documents that prove the British government legally bought the sculptures. Besides, they say, art doesn't belong to a country. If the British museum returns the marbles to Greece, museums around the world would have to return all kinds of art to their original countries. Museums could be left bare.

TFK Ruined Ruins

How do you dust off ancient artworks? Very carefully. But in the 1930s, the British Museum botched the cleaning of the Elgin Marbles. A British aristocrat, Lord Duveen, thought the sculptures could use some touching up. Since he was paying for a new gallery to house the marbles, workers at the museum obeyed his wishes. They started scrubbing down the antiquities with metal scrapers.

The cleaning caused major damage. Original paint was removed, and the marbles' surfaces were ground down. When museum curators realized what had happened, they used stained wax to recolor some of the marbles and to cover up their mistake. Over the years, people forgot about the cleaning controversy—until, that is, marble expert William St. Clair dug around to see what he could uncover about the cover-up.

St. Clair says 80 percent of the marbles' surfaces and paint are lost forever. He also notes that sculpture marks made by the original artists from the fifth century B.C. have been smoothed out. That's because the museum cleaners used wire brushes and copper chisels to scrub the marbles.

In the mid-1990s, a Greek team of archaeologists, conservationists, and chemical engineers used new techniques to study the marbles in the British Museum. Their four-day investigation showed what artists around the world feared: the ancient ruins were ruined! Their surface was so deeply scraped that the marbles' pores had been exposed. Dirt and mold had crept into the crevices. The marbles' form and color were so badly damaged that there was no hope of restoring them to their original condition. The Elgin Marbles on display in the British Museum today look quite different from the way they did when they were on the Parthenon.

In 1829 when Greece won its freedom from the Ottoman Empire, the Greeks began rebuilding their fallen monuments. The first monument to be patched up was the Parthenon. During a victory celebration in 1834, two Parthenon columns were re-erected. In 1835 the Acropolis was declared a national monument. After 1835 nothing from the site—not even a pebble—was allowed to be removed from the grounds. That stopped the looters and souvenir hunters. In 1847 a special museum was finally set up to house the fragments of the Acropolis monuments. People could no longer harm the buildings or the fallen pieces.

Still, nature took its toll on the structures left standing on the Acropolis. A big earthquake in 1894 shook many pieces to the ground and threatened to topple the entire Parthenon. The building held strong. Not taking any chances, the Greek government hired an architect to restore the monument to its original condition. The plan worked—except for one little detail. The architect used iron bars to hold together the broken columns. The iron rusted—and burst the columns.

In the 1960s air pollution was a big problem for Athens and the Parthenon. Pollution in the air created acid rain that destroyed the surface of every piece of marble. Within a few years, the pollution did more damage to the Parthenon than any other event in its history, even Lord Elgin's removal of the marbles. The Greek government had to act fast. It set up the Committee for the Conservation of the Acropolis Monuments, a group of experts whose main mission was to reverse the damage and save what was left.

Since the mid-1980s, scaffolds have become part of the scenery of the Acropolis. Teams of artists and archaeologists have been repairing and restoring broken marble on the buildings. So far, the committee has transferred original sculptures to a museum and replaced them with casts. That helps protect the sculptures from further damage. Restoring the Parthenon is a complicated process that could take decades more to finish.

The Nashville Parthenon?

You don't have to travel to Greece or to England to see parts of the Parthenon. Just head to Nashville, Tennessee. The city is the home of the only exact replica of the ancient building. Visitors can see the entire building as it may have originally looked—complete with a copy of the Athena statue that mysteriously disappeared 700 years after it was created. Its statue of Athena, which stands more than 41 feet (12 m) tall, is the largest piece of indoor sculpture in the United States.

Athena

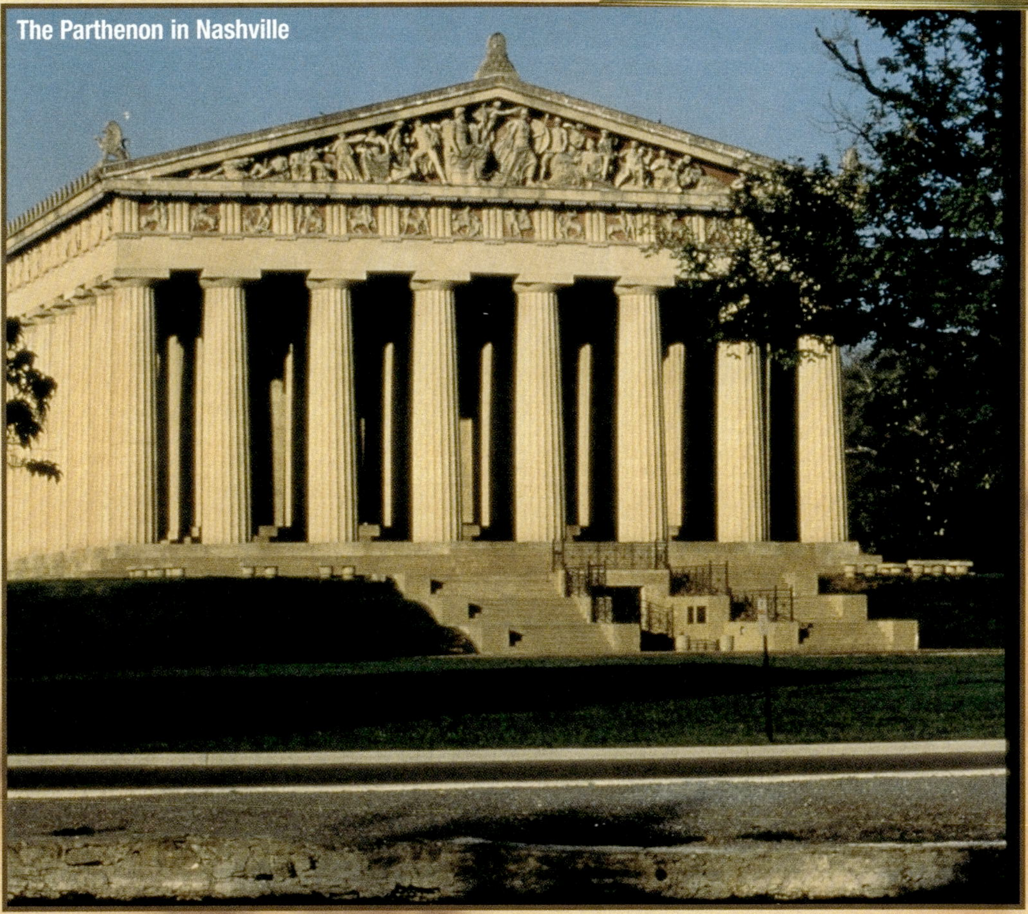

The Parthenon in Nashville

ELGIN'S

Why did Lord Elgin want to collect Greek art? Take a look at these pieces, from the British Museum's collection, to see for yourself.

Standing more than 25 feet (8 m) tall, this column was part of a group that once held up the roof of the Erechtheion, a temple that was a shrine to Greek gods.

COLLECTION

Some historians believe that this scene shows the Great Panathenaic Festival—a celebration held every four years to honor the goddess Athena.

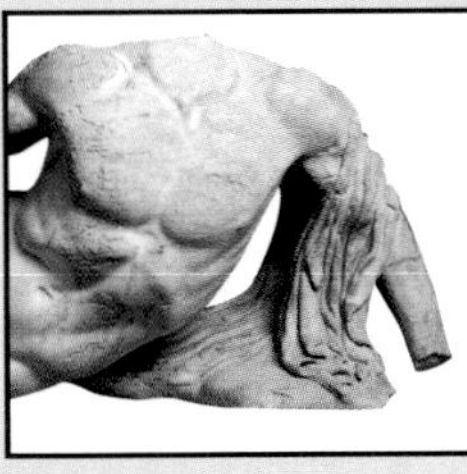

This figure of a river god once sat on the west pediment, or triangle that forms the end of the roof, of the Parthenon. It looked on as the figures of Athena and Poseidon, two Greek gods, fought over Athens and its surrounding lands.

Mythical battles, like the one below between a human and a centaur, were sculpted along the Parthenon's frieze, or decorated border. The mythical centaurs were creatures that were half human and half horse.

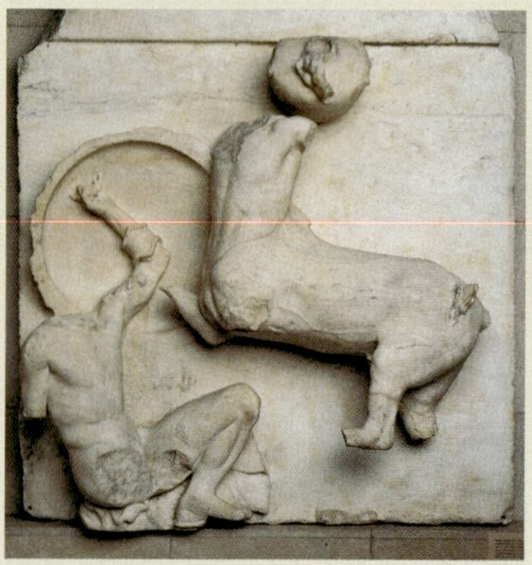

TFK

A Poet's Vision

John Keats, a British poet, wrote this poem. What inspired him? The title says it all.

from *On Seeing the Elgin Marbles for the First Time*

My spirit is too
weak; mortality
Weighs heavily on me
like unwilling sleep,
And each imagined pinnacle and steep
Of godlike hardship tells me I must die
Like a sick eagle looking at the sky.
Yet 'tis a gentle luxury to weep,
That I have not the cloudy winds to keep
Fresh for the opening of the morning's eye.

The east pediment of the Parthenon showed the story of the birth of Athena. The goddesses Hestia, Dione, and Aphrodite (below) looked on as Athena sprang, fully-grown, from the head of Zeus, her father. This statue is one of the few sculptures to survive from the badly damaged east pediment.

Alongside the figures of Athena and Poseidon on the west pediment were their messengers: Athena's Hermes and Poseidon's Iris (shown here).

These female figures hold up the roof of the Erechtheion's porch. They are called the caryatids—named for the young women of Sparta who danced in honor of Artemis, goddess of the hunt and wild animals. Lord Elgin removed one of the caryatids, which is on display at the British Museum. The other five caryatids remain in Greece.

This statue of Dionysos, the god of song, once adorned the east pediment of the Parthenon.

TFK DID YOU KNOW

Behind the Scenes at the Parthenon

The Acropolis has always been Athens' sacred hill. Palaces, temples, and civic buildings sat atop the Acropolis, overlooking the city below. But the Acropolis was badly damaged during a war with the Persians. Athenians defeated the Persians in 479 B.C.

Pericles, Athens' new leader, wanted to re-energize his citizens and show off his city's power. He envisioned a new Acropolis with buildings that were grander than anything ever built. To turn his vision into reality, Pericles hired Phidias, the best sculptor of that time. Beginning in 447 B.C., with the help of architects Ictinus and Callicrates, Phidias completed the Parthenon in 438 B.C. There was much more to the Parthenon than its famous marbles. Here's an inside look at the ancient monument.

20 grooves in each column

Though they appear to be made of one huge chunk of marble, the columns are constructed in sections called *drums.* Square plugs in the center of each drum hold the columns together.

Bright colors once adorned the Parthenon. The triglyphs, blocks with vertical grooves, were dark blue and some of the other parts of the frieze were red. The backgrounds of the metope sculptures were painted various colors, and the eyes, lips, and hair of metope figures were tinted.

8 columns on each narrow side
17 columns on each long side
Made of Pentelic marble, a white-colored marble brought from Mount Pentelicus near Athens
228 feet (69 m) long, 104 feet (32 m) wide

TFK DID YOU KNOW

Did Elgin Save the Marbles?

If Elgin's team wanted to take away already-broken fragments of the Parthenon, it would have had lots to choose from. Over the centuries the Parthenon has faced damage, destruction, and change. The first change to the temple occurred in A.D. 450. In that year the temple was turned into a Christian church. Many sculptures were removed from inside the temple to make room for an altar. A colossal gold-and-ivory statue of Athena that once stood in the center of the building vanished. During the Middle Ages, many figures were vandalized, making some sculptures unrecognizable. In the late 1600s, Ottoman soldiers used the Parthenon to store gunpowder. In 1687 Venetian troops bombed the Parthenon during a war with the Ottoman Empire. The gunpowder exploded, damaging the walls and the roof.

During the 18th and 19th centuries, classical Greek art became very popular. Tourists wanted keepsakes from Greece, so they snapped off noses, fingers, and toes from classical Greek sculptures. Other European governments also wanted to add to their collections of classical Greek art. It was rumored that some countries, such as France, were planning to seize the Acropolis and remove everything on it. Lord Elgin wanted to remove as much Greek art from the Acropolis as possible before other collectors had a chance to do the same. His team filled up 200 chests with artifacts and loaded them onto a ship bound for England. At last, Elgin thought, he had saved the sculptures! They would be forever preserved and protected in England.

Some historians think Lord Elgin damaged the Parthenon more than anyone else. Had he not taken the sculptures, they say, the Parthenon would have had a good chance of staying intact. Did Lord Elgin save the marbles from destruction? Or did he only add to the damage to the Parthenon? What do you think?